LANDSCAPES OF THE RIBBLE

LANDSCAPES OF THE RIBBLE

Andy Latham

F

FRANCES LINCOLN LIMITED
PUBLISHERS

Frances Lincoln Ltd
4 Torriano Mews
Torriano Avenue
London NW5 2RZ
www.franceslincoln.com

Landscapes of the Ribble
Copyright © Frances Lincoln Limited 2010
Text and photographs copyright © Andy Latham 2010
First Frances Lincoln edition 2010

British Library Cataloguing-in-Publication data
A catalogue record for this book is available from the British Library.

ISBN: 978-0-7112-3028-6

Printed and bound in Singapore

9 8 7 6 5 4 3 2 1

PAGE 1 *Early morning, Marshside*: The Ribble estuary is of international importance as a wetland habitat. While cars speed past on the coast road to Southport, another world exists on the landward side at the RSPB reserve of Marshside.

PAGE 2–3 *Winter dawn, Pendle Hill, Hurst Green*

ABOVE *Slash of light, Smearsett Scar*: I braved some heavy weather to ascend Smearsett Scar knowing that if the weather broke there could be something spectacular. I wasn't disappointed as a shaft of sunlight briefly broke through to light up the slopes of Pen-y-Ghent.

To Michelle, of course

CONTENTS

INTRODUCTION

The Ribble

Deep in the heart of the Yorkshire Dales, a trickle of water emerges from a tiny wall of limestone, creates a soggy patch of grass and moss, disappears for a while until finally forming a recognisable stream. This is Jam Sike, the source of the delightful River Ribble.

Over the next 70 miles, the river flows through some of the finest landscapes in the north of England, from the austere heights of the Yorkshire Dales Three Peaks country, through the lush green Ribble Valley beneath brooding Pendle Hill, and on to its estuary, which is internationally-important for its wildlife, between Southport and Lytham St. Anne's. In *Landscapes of the Ribble* I hope to give you a visual flavour of this grand journey, from familiar vistas to hidden gems.

The first few miles are all windswept moor and solitude, as a succession of gills including Long Gill join forces to create Gayle Beck. Sometimes the beck flows gently over a wide boulder bed, sometimes it is squeezed through miniature limestone gorges, before it finally emerges at Ribblehead, the great mountain amphitheatre of the Dales.

This is great walking country with three long distance footpaths, the Pennine Way, the Dales Way and the Ribble Way passing nearby, while the famous Three Peaks of Whernside, Ingleborough and Pen-y-Ghent, all vie for attention. Ribblehead Viaduct, the epitome of Victorian engineering, is dwarfed by the surrounding grandeur. Facts about the construction of the viaduct and the Blea Moor tunnel on the Settle to Carlisle railway line, are full of superlatives, and it is impossible to imagine the hardships of the 'navvies' working in such a harsh environment, for only a tough beauty now remains.

Flowing south, the river first acquires its name as it passes below the Ingleborough massif. Limestone now begins to dominate the scenery all the way to Settle. Caves, pot holes, sink holes and limestone pavements are now the order of the day, as the river wanders slowly through the glaciated valley.

The Ingleborough National Nature Reserve was created to protect much of this precious landscape of clints and grikes, moss and fern, hawthorn and rowan. Beneath this fascinating landscape is a dramatic secret world of caves and passages that can be only hinted at to walkers like myself, at openings like Long Churn Cave and Alum Pot, a cauldron of thundering water, rising mist and impenetrable darkness.

At Horton-in-Ribblesdale, Pen-y-Ghent transfixes the eye, which is just as well given that across the valley vast quarries eat away at Moughton's eastern slopes – a real case of Beauty and the Beast. Pen-y-Ghent is undoubtedly the finest peak in the Dales, its distinctive profile being a highlight of the Pennine Way, as well as offering the challenge of many walkers' first experience of climbing a big hill. Wherever one wanders in Ribblesdale, it seems that Pen-y-Ghent will be somewhere in the background.

Beyond Horton the landscape softens a little, becoming the typical Dales' limestone scenery of fields, barns and shapely hills. But great views and attractive villages abound. By now the Ribble is quite substantial, and at Stainforth, there are its only major falls, a great place to spot salmon leaping in the late autumn.

Nearby Settle, the first major settlement encountered by the river, is a lovely market town famous for being the terminus of the Settle-Carlisle railway. Settle is also well-known for its wonderfully-named 'Ye Olde Naked Man Café' – named after the figure carved on the datestone for the building (which had to be covered up when Queen Victoria visited). Above the town in Victoria Cave, the remains of rhinoceroses, hippopotamuses and elephants were discovered, evidence of the inhabitants of the area during an inter-glacial period 120,000 years ago.

Once Settle's hills are left behind, the valley opens up, with the fells of the Forest of Bowland appearing to the west and Pendle Hill already beginning to dominate to the south. Between Rathmell and Long Preston the meandering river frequently floods, providing a valuable habitat for waders such as lapwing and redshank.

As the river begins a slow turn to the west it enters Lancashire, and the name of the valley changes from Ribblesdale to that of the Ribble Valley. The landscape becomes one of rolling green countryside and picturesque villages, such as Bolton-by-Bowland, Waddington and Downham, while all the while, Pendle Hill gets bigger and bigger. History abounds in the medieval churches and old manor houses, the ruined abbeys at Sawley and Whalley, and the even older remains of a Roman fort at Ribchester. This is Lancashire at its finest, and a real eye-opener for those who think the county is one big Lowry painting.

Pendle Hill is omnipresent in the Ribble Valley, rising in splendid isolation, and forming a separate part of the Forest of Bowland AONB. It will forever be associated with the infamous 17th century witch trials, but it deserves more than that, for it is a grand hill of great character. All approaches are steep and the moorland plateau is a wild place for much of the year. The views are inspirational, and indeed George Fox had a vision on Pendle which led to his establishment of the Quaker movement. Even if you simply potter around the base of the hill, you can't fail to be impressed by its presence.

The political centre of the Ribble Valley is the attractive town of Clitheroe, dominated by its medieval castle keep and, of course, Pendle Hill. It has a growing reputation for its range of independent food retailers and is the centre of the Ribble Valley Food Trail.

A short distance south-west of Clitheroe, the Ribble is boosted by the confluence of its two main tributaries, within less than a mile of each other. These are the Hodder, having descended from the heart of the Forest of Bowland to the north, and the Calder, from the hills above Burnley, to the south-east. The grand building of Stonyhurst College presides over this section, while rising behind is the aptly-named Longridge Fell, with its acres of forestry plantations and stunning views across the Vale of Chipping towards the Bowland Fells. More natural pockets of semi-ancient woodland are also a key feature of the landscape, as the river passes Ribchester right up to the outskirts of Preston.

England's newest city barely notices the river as it slips by on its southern outskirts, although a huge dock basin was created in the late 19th century and Preston had a brief spell as a major sea port. The last few miles pass through a flat landscape of salt marsh, drainage channels, reclaimed land and mud till the river finally reaches the Irish Sea at the 10-mile wide estuary.

This inter-tidal environment of sand, silt, saltmarsh and mud make the Ribble estuary of international importance as a wildfowl habitat and since 1979, a large portion has been designated a National Nature Reserve, managed by Natural England. The Royal Society for the Protection of Birds also manage a reserve with several public hides at Marshside, at the southern end of the estuary, and are also letting the sea reclaim Hesketh Out Marsh in order to create new habitats.

The northern terminus of the river is the delightful twin town of Lytham St Anne's, a seaside town that oozes a quiet charm which is the complete antithesis of its big brother Blackpool, just up the road. It is a fitting finale for a landscape which never disappoints and frequently entrances – a landscape which quietly and gently enriches the soul.

The source of the Ribble

The Book

Several years ago I moved to north Bolton and made a conscious decision to start exploring more of Lancashire, rather than my usual trips to Scotland or the Lakes. I quickly recognised the merits of the Ribble Valley and so began a personal project to photograph its landscapes. I continued adding to my portfolio on and off for a few years but it wasn't until I walked the Ribble Way that the thought actually occurred to me to develop the idea into covering the whole length of the river, from the wild beauty of the Three Peaks all the way to the sea at genteel Lytham St. Annes.

The concept appealed firstly as it was a genuine journey, exploring the changing landscape of a single valley and secondly, as it combined my favourite part of the Yorkshire Dales, Ribblesdale, with the beloved county of my birth, Lancashire.

People tend to compartmentalise the land into distinct regions, yet on the ground there is no sign of such change. It simply flows effortlessly, ignoring successive political boundaries. When out walking I enjoy reaching a viewpoint and seeking out places I know, joining them together to build up my picture of the bigger landscape, which in turn strengthens my connection to the land, my sense of place.

The book is not meant to be a documentary of the river valley but is merely my interpretation of the landscape, taking the kind of photographs that I like to take. Another photographer would no doubt take a very different set of images, and indeed, if I were to repeat the project I'm sure very little would stay the same. While I planned to take particular subjects and views, I frequently found myself photographing something quite different. I like to take my time at a location and spend hours ambling around to get a feel for the place. The weather, light, season, time of day, my own mood, all influence what images are taken and that unpredictability and lack of control over the land are part of the joy of being a landscape photographer.

For images to be successful the photographer has to have some connection to the subject, whether that is a fascination, admiration, sense of wonder, memory or some other emotional tie. Consequently there are few images of the towns along the river – I simply don't get excited about them and therefore struggle to make interesting images. I also apologise if I have omitted your own favourite location or viewpoint; there are plenty of places that I still haven't visited or it could be that when I went the conditions weren't right or inspiration failed me.

My wish, when you view the book, is that I may surprise you with the variety and beauty of the landscape that the river has helped to create. If you are not familiar with the Ribble, hopefully you may be inspired enough to make a visit, and even if you have walked extensively in the region, I hope that my work provides you with an even greater appreciation of the landscape. Maybe, even, the next time you are exploring your local landscape, wherever that may be, you might pause for a moment and recognise the wonder that is all around us, if only we care to look for it.

Cam Fell to Stainforth — Three Peaks Country

Might over Matter, Ribblehead Viaduct: One of the most famous structures in the Yorkshire Dales, Ribblehead Viaduct crosses Batty Moss – a symbol of Victorian engineering overcoming common sense. Facts and statistics about its construction contain many superlatives yet it is dwarfed by the immense scenery at Ribblehead, crossing the valley between Whernside and Ingleborough.

Open spaces, Gayle Moor: The Ribble Way descends alongside Jam Sike on Gayle Moor. These are lonely windswept slopes, with the only sign of habitation being the distant Newby Head Farm.

Crumbling opportunity, Gayle Beck Lodge and Ingleborough: Jam Sike becomes Long Gill, which in turn becomes Gayle Beck, which flows past Gayle Beck Lodge. This former shooting lodge is a familiar sight for travellers along the B6255, but my efforts to photograph it in previous years had failed due to uninspiring light. I finally chose a nice morning to visit only to discover that half of the building had fallen down!

Morning drama, Ingleborough, Ribblehead: Small outcrops of limestone pavement at Ribblehead provide excellent views of Park Fell, Simon Fell and Ingleborough. My morning excursion didn't yield the hoped-for sunrise of raking light, instead I was presented with a scene of brooding menace. I almost expected an alien mother-ship to emerge from those clouds.

Stream, sheep, Ribblehead Viaduct and Whernside: A small tributary of the Ribble runs beneath the road junction at Ribblehead. A wide-angle lens exaggerates the water while diminishing the viaduct.

Time for reflection, Ribblehead Quarry: This quarry lies just across the track from Ribblehead Station and is a real gem of a place. Abandoned as a working quarry in 1958, it is now managed by Natural England as part of the Ingleborough National Nature Reserve. A fascinating waymarked walk explores how nature has reclaimed such a bare landscape, and how it also includes the remains of a Viking settlement.

Late morning, Soft rock, Park Fell, Gauber Rocks: Limestone pavement is an addictive subject and I always get excited when I encounter it. However making a successful photograph usually requires finding a section that provides a pleasant flow or pattern, which is more difficult than you may think. Here Park Fell and Ingleborough play second fiddle to the lovely texture of the rock.

Rock ribs, Whernside from Gauber Rocks: In conditions of drifting light patience is required, waiting for the light to fall in the right places. When using large format equipment, repeated shots are out of the question, you simply have to hold your nerve, remain optimistic, and hope that you've not let an opportunity slip by.

Whernside, Hawthorn, Limestone, Colt Park: I am constantly surprised by how quickly conditions can change. Pottering around Colt Park on an overcast evening, the cloud started to disperse and within twenty minutes, these tiny wisps were all that remained.

Greenery, Ling Gill: Walkers on the Pennine Way will pass the impressive wooded chasm of Ling Gill, a National Nature Reserve managed by Natural England.

Gentle swell, Gauber: Between Ribblehead and Selside the valley is filled with soft rounded hills, deposited by a retreating glacier. In these misty conditions, these hills seemed almost fluid.

Fungi and stream, Selside: This stream has a brief spell above ground before disappearing into Upper Long Churn Cave, part of the Alum Pot system. Alum Pot is arguably Britain's finest pothole – 120 feet long, 35 feet wide and with a waterfall plunging 200 feet into the darkness.

Giant crater, Hull Pot: Across the valley from Alum Pot, Hull Pot is equally spectacular, being 300 feet long, 60 feet wide and 60 feet deep. The waterfall only occurs after periods of very wet weather but amazingly it has been known to fill entirely with water – a photograph from the 1960's showing this can be seen in the Pen-y-Ghent Café in Horton.

Limestone pavement, Borrins Moor

Fleeting light, Moughton: Moughton is a fine hill neglected by many, probably because of the vast quarries on its eastern slopes. However the summit slopes are a sheer delight of limestone pavements and juniper gullies, with grand views across Crummackdale towards Ingleborough. Strong winds made life very difficult with the large format camera, and it was a test of patience waiting for a lull to coincide with some interesting light.

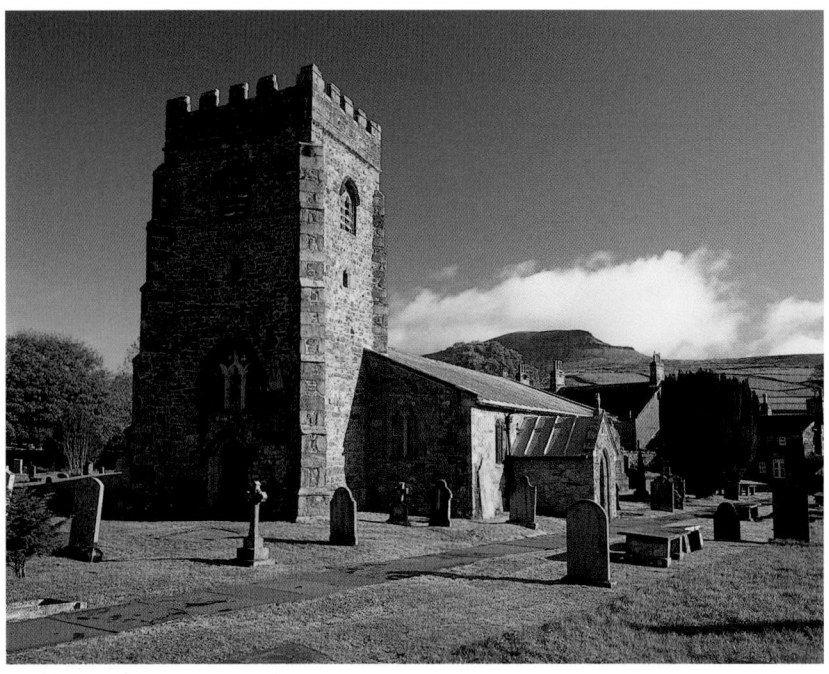

St Oswald's, Horton-in-Ribblesdale: You will soon notice that I have a weakness for attractive churches, there being several examples in the book. There are so many picturesque churches along the river's journey that I could probably fill a book with them (now there's a thought!).

Golden colours, River Ribble, near Horton

October morning, River Ribble, Pen-y-Ghent, near Horton

Stormy light, Pen-y-Ghent, Dale Head: The Pennine Way leads on from Dale Head towards Pen-y-Ghent. Showery conditions lent themselves perfectly to some selective lighting for extra drama.

Studfold Moss, Helwith Bridge

Vanishing hillside, Dry Rigg Quarry, Helwith Bridge: There is very little industry along the Ribble apart from quarrying. Moughton has three huge scars on the eastern slopes – Dry Rigg produces slate for road surfacing and Arcow quarries limestone. There's no escaping the rumble of lorries on the B6479.

Moody morning, Pen-y-Ghent, Fountains Fell: Fountains Fell is the poor relation of Pen-y-Ghent, rarely visited except by those on the Pennine Way. However its empty slopes reward those willing to venture off the beaten track with fine views of much of the Dales.

Two trees, Moughton and Ingleborough, Feizor Nick: A cloudless, hazy morning killed any prospects for a grand view towards Ingleborough, and I knew something closer at hand would be needed to take advantage of the warm light.

Autumn evening, Stainforth: Stainforth stands quietly back from the main road and has a fine collection of stone-built cottages. Footpaths radiate in all directions for it is in the centre of fine walking territory. Pendle Hill makes an early appearance in the distance.

Sunlit barn, Smearsett Scar, Stainforth: Another instance when drifting light spotlit the focus of my composition.

Stainforth to Gisburn

Heavenly light, Winskill: Sometimes the beauty of the light can be truly astounding, and it is the privilege of a landscape photographer to have the opportunity to experience such moments.

Stainforth Force, Stainforth: A series of cascades and an ancient packhorse bridge, owned by the National Trust, make this an idyllic picnic spot. In late autumn you can also be treated to the spectacular sight of leaping salmon, as they make their way upstream to spawn.

Swirling maelstrom, Catrigg Force: Less well-known than Stainforth Force, Catrigg is reached via a steep pull up from Stainforth. It hides in a dramatic little gorge and is well worth the effort of the climb.

Winding road, Winskill: Winskill is a fabulous location, combining great views of Moughton, Ingleborough and Smearsett Scar with the more intimate pleasures of limestone pavements and twisted hawthorns. Add in a picture-perfect distant farmhouse and you can have hours of fun waiting for the right light.

OPPOSITE
TOP *Wall, Barn, Two trees, Langcliffe:* A simple scene, quintessentially the Dales.
BOTTOM *Two gates, Stainforth Scar, Langcliffe*

Lost monument, Langcliffe: Between Langcliffe and Stainforth there are some unassuming industrial remains of quarrying and lime production beneath Stainforth Scar. The best preserved building is the Hoffman limekiln, not much to look at from the outside but once you brave the interior, your eyes adjust to the darkness and a vault of cathedral proportions is revealed. An extraordinary and secret place.

Snowdrops and the church of St John the Evangelist, Langcliffe

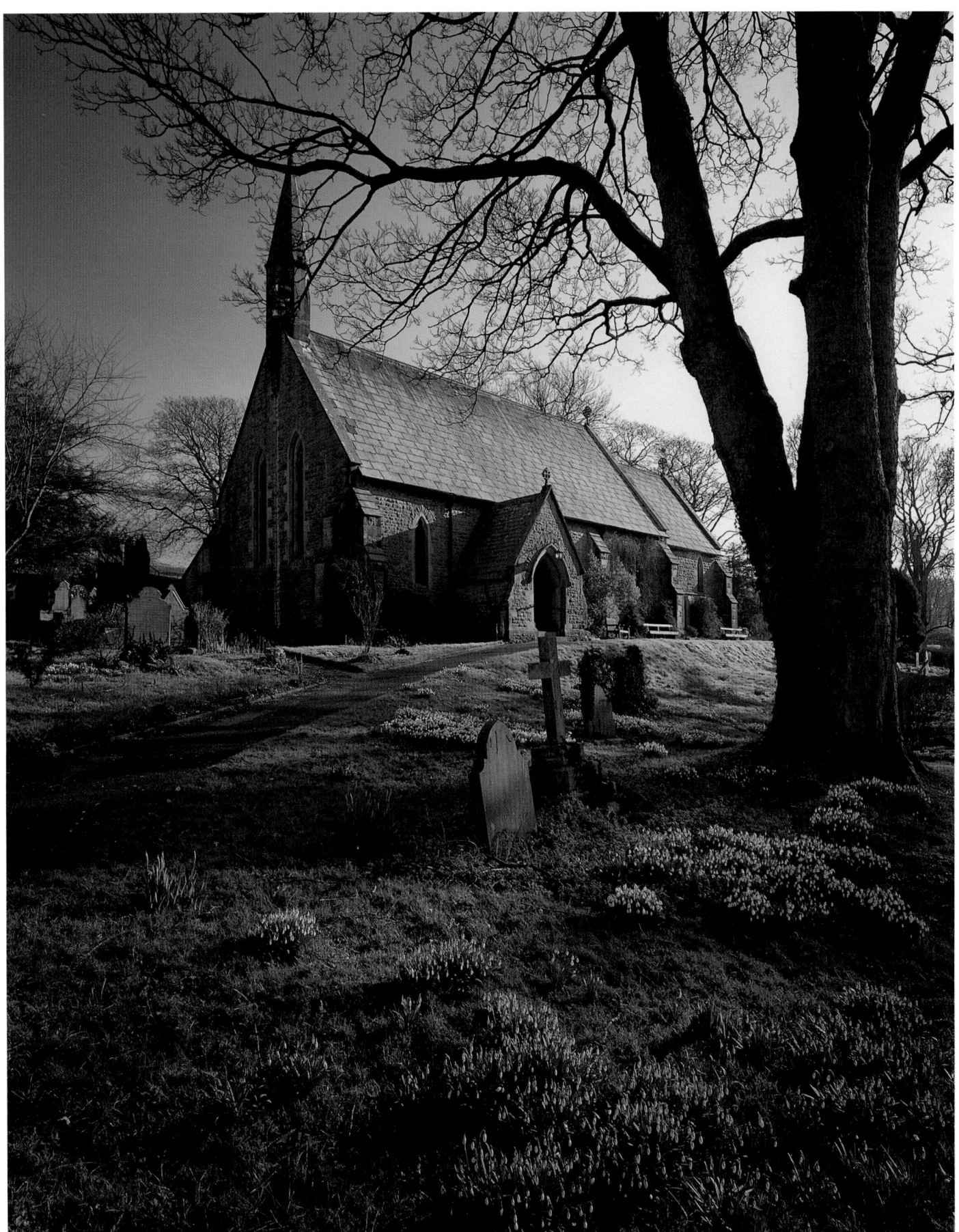

Rooftops at dusk, Settle: Famous for being the eastern terminus of the Settle-Carlisle railway, Settle is an attractive small market town and the first settlement of any size along the Ribble. Behind the market square looms Castleberg Hill, a limestone crag topped by a flag pole, which offers great views over the town.

OPPOSITE *Warrendale Knotts, Settle*: This shapely collection of crags only became open to walkers following its designation as Open Access land in 2004.

Pen-y-Ghent and Victoria Cave, Warrendale Knotts: Excavated in 1837 (Queen Victoria's coronation year) and subsequently enlarged, Victoria Cave yielded many fine discoveries including the bones of hyenas, rhinoceroses, elephants and hippopotamuses, all evidence of an inter-glacial warm period.

Cleatop Park, Settle:
This patch of ancient woodland has recently been added to, thanks to the work of the Woodland Trust and the Yorkshire Dales Millennium Trust which have planted a broad range of new trees. Hidden among the saplings, below the older wood, is a Bronze Age burial mound.

Glistening branches, Scaleber

Soft light, Curious cattle, Coney Garth

Wall, Barn, Fading frost, Giggleswick: Giggleswick lies across the river from Settle and, apart from being a very attractive village, is notable for the renowned public school, founded in the early sixteenth century.

Cocket Moss, near Rathmell

Frosty morning, Whelpstone Crag: Whelpstone Crag is a prominent flat-topped hill on the edge of the Forest of Bowland. Few people venture to this side of the valley, so it is a quiet place of small crags and sweeping views.

Ribble Ings: Between Settle and Long Preston, the Ribble meanders through a wide floodplain which provides a valuable habitat for waders such as lapwing and redshank. The best views are from the A65 but finding a location to photograph from proved trickier than expected and I ended up high above Long Preston for this shot.

Flood, Rathmell: Heavy overnight rain closed the road between Settle and Rathmell and transformed the valley below, the waters of the floodplain extending further than usual.

Buttercup meadow, Rathmell: Rathmell sits on the wrong side of the river to attract many visitors, which is a shame as the quiet lanes and paths are well worth exploring.

Early morning, Little Newton, Long Preston: A dozen deer kept a close eye on me
from the hill above as I waited for the sun to strike the bridge.

Frosty gate, Distant Pendle, Long Preston

St Mary the Virgin, Long Preston

Castle Haugh, Paythorne: A large wooded mound is visible to motorists along the road between Gisburn and Paythorne. This is Castle Haugh, the site of a Norman motte and bailey castle perched on top of a steep bank above a large bend in the river. I'd tried on several occasions to capture some sense of the castle, but eventually settled on a detail of the woodland with the meander barely visible through the trees.

Gentle flow, Halton Bridge

Spring sunshine, Halton Bridge:
Cows, fresh out of the milking
parlour, found me and my
equipment very interesting
as I set up for this shot on a
bright May morning.

Gisburn to Clitheroe

Bracken, Heather, Pendle, from Bradford Fell: The hills north of Clitheroe have numerous names and one merges seamlessly into another. They all share great views to Pendle, colourful swathes of purple heather and vibrant green mosses – just watch out for the midges in the summer!

Feeding circle, Weets Hill, Bracewell: Weets is an unassuming hill above Barnoldswick with some of the grandest views of Ribble country and beyond. Needless to say Pendle Hill dominates, but the Three Peaks dot the horizon, the lush pastures fill the valley and the broader sweeps of Lancashire lie to the south.

BELOW *Distant views, Weets Hill*: The view towards Blacko Tower and Colne from the summit of Weets Hill. Looking at the photograph later with a magnifier, I was struck by how many wind turbines could be seen – the shape of things to come on northern uplands if we are not careful.

The Old Courthouse, Bolton-by-Bowland: Bolton-by Bowland is an extremely pretty and historical village that was recorded in the Domesday Book. The church of St Peter and St Paul should not be missed if you happen to stop by.

Ancient cross base, Bolton-by-Bowland

Moonrise over Pendle,
Sawley

Summer evening, Rimmington

Sawley Abbey: Founded by Cistercian monks in 1147, Sawley Abbey suffered badly following the Dissolution and its abbot was hanged for supporting the Pilgrimage of Grace. Now managed by English Heritage, the ruins are a real gem in a beautiful corner of the Ribble.

Fallen tree, Twiston: As I set up for this photograph, two deer bounded past within a few metres of me, as startled by my presence as I was by theirs.

April snow, Pendle Hill, Hill Foot

Bright winter morning, Pendle Hill, Stang Top Moor: I make no apologies for the number of times that Pendle Hill appears in this book because for me, Pendle Hill is *the* hill of the valley. It is visible from viewpoints along virtually the whole length of the river and totally dominates large sections of the Ribble Valley. Wherever you walk it is somewhere in the background, a great whaleback brooding in the clouds. Its fame stretches well beyond the north-west for its associations with the witch trials of 1612, yet there is also a more spiritual connection as George Fox had a vision on Pendle which led to his foundation of the Quaker movement.

View from Pendle: In the distance are the Bowland Fells, Whernside and Ingleborough; Bradford and Grindleford Fells lie across the valley; Worsaw Hill is the mound on the left with Downham hidden in shadow.

Pendle Hill and Downham

Worsaw Farm: Worsaw Farm beneath Pendle was the location for the classic
1960's film *Whistle Down the Wind*.

Cold evening, Smoking chimney, Worsaw: The cement works at Clitheroe is a bigger landmark than its castle – wherever you go it is always somewhere in the background and sometimes the mood of the day suits its inclusion in a view.

Grouse butt, Bradford Fell

Heather, Bradford Fell

Moss, Far Brown Hill

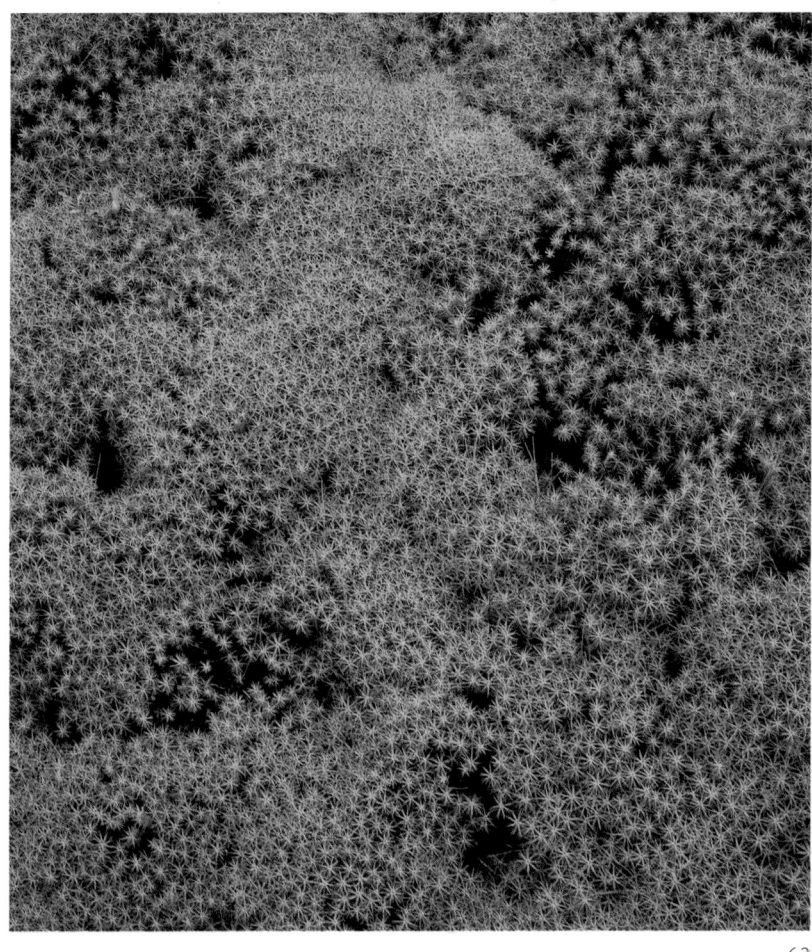

Spring morning, Waddington: The Coronation Gardens shown here are not the only attractive feature of Waddington, for further up the village are the Widows' Hospital and eighteenth century almshouses. Opposite the village is Waddington Hall, where Henry VI lived for a year during the Wars of the Roses.

Clearing mist, Dozing heron, Bradford Bridge: I've lost count of the number of herons that I have startled on my wanderings during this project, and I never cease to be amazed by their presence. As a child they always seemed such a rare and exotic bird and sightings were always treasured. Sadly, I only had my landscape kit with me so the heron is a mere speck on the photo, but it remains prominent in my memory of a beautiful morning.

Sunrise over Clitheroe: Clitheroe is a charming town dominated by a fine small castle. I had hoped to include an image or two of the castle and the views from its walls but sadly scaffolding on the keep and restoration work prevented me.

Clitheroe to Longridge

Heavy frost, Busy sheep, near Whalley

Sparkling water, near Eadsford Bridge

Swaying cotton grass above Sabden, Pendle Hill: One of the great delights of moorland in the spring is the swathes of cotton grass bobbing in the wind – a fairy-tale element to a landscape that can appear bleak.

*Carpet of ramsons,
Spring Wood*

Springtime, Whalley Abbey gardens: A tranquil place among the ruins of the Cistercian Abbey founded in 1296. Much larger than nearby Sawley Abbey, the finest features are the two remaining gatehouses.

Quiet morning, early autumn, Hacking Wood

Mitton Wood

End of the day, Hacking Hall: The River Calder joins the Ribble at Hacking Hall and up until the 1950's there was a passenger ferry across the river. As absolutely glorious light bathed Whalley Nab to my left, but refused to strike where I was, I regretted my decision to shoot from here. I waited and waited for some light till at last a touch of pink appeared in the frame as dusk set in.

Pendle and Clitheroe from Birdy Brow, Longridge Fell: A minor road climbs up Kemple End from Mitton and at a disused quarry, the Ribble Valley is revealed in all its glory. Between sharp rain showers the sun occasionally lit the valley like a giant searchlight.

Gathering gloom, Stonyhurst College, Hurst Green: Regarded as one of the finest schools in the country, and arguably the finest building of the Ribble, parts of Stonyhurst date back to the fourteenth century and Oliver Cromwell is reputed to have stayed a night before the Battle of Preston. The college and Hurst Green have connections with Tolkein and as much of the surrounding area is alleged to have been inspiration for elements of *The Lord of the Rings* a dark atmosphere seemed appropriate. The building and gardens are open to the public in the summer.

Evening sunlight above the Ribble

Dinckley Bridge,
Hurst Green

Blustery spring, Marles Wood

Burning gold, Sale Wheel: At Marles Wood the Ribble passes through a mini gorge and makes a sharp right turn, forming a whirlpool known as Sale Wheel.

Water slide, Duddel Brook

St Wilfred's, Ribchester: Ribchester is a fascinating village full of historical interest. It was the site of the Roman fort of *Bremetennacum*, which guarded an important river crossing, and relics can be seen in the museum by the church, which is built over a corner of the fort.

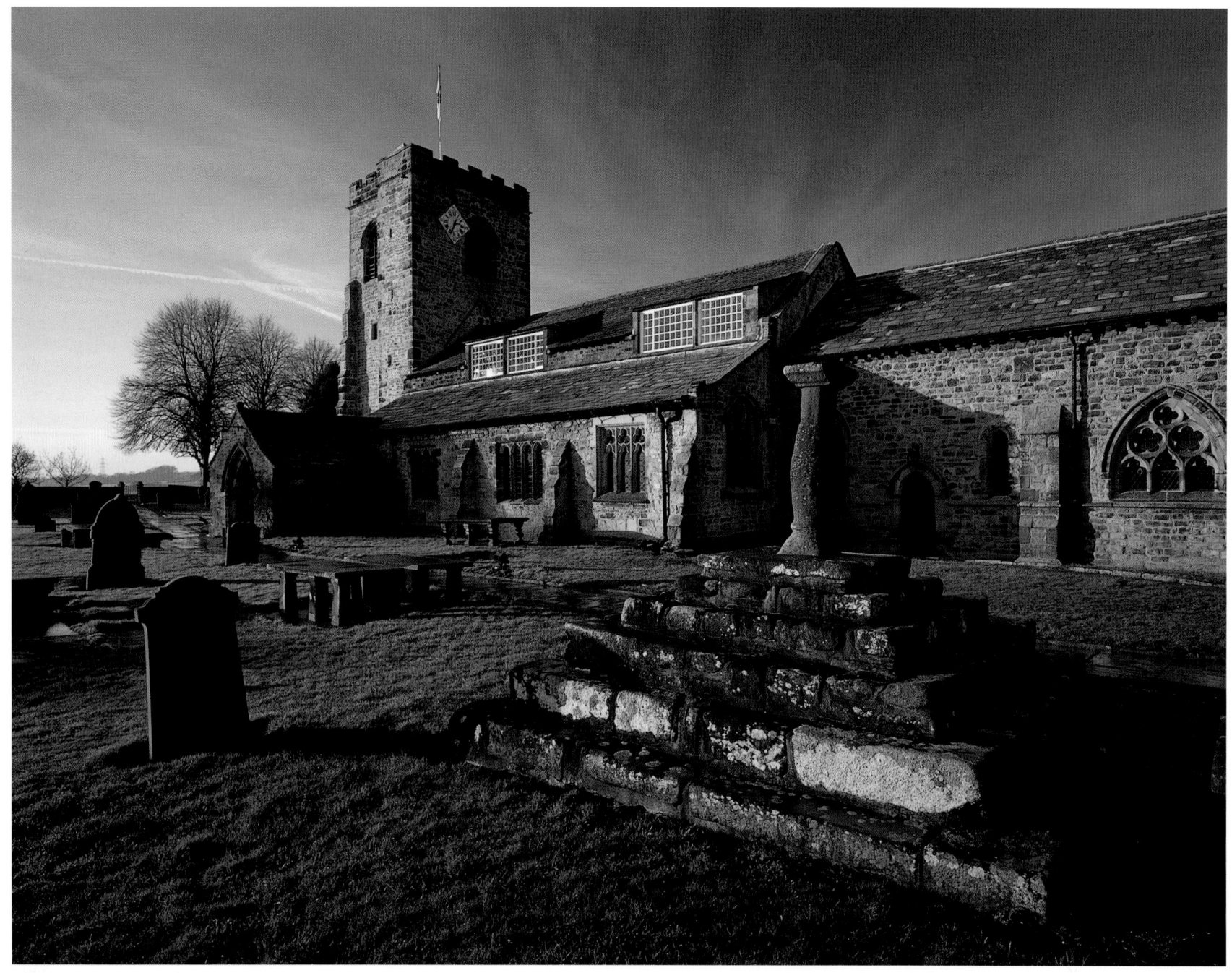

Big bend, Ribchester

Blustery afternoon, Mercyfield Wood, Osbaldeston

Cluttered summit, Mellor Moor: Mellor Moor holds quite a commanding view of the Ribble Valley and consequently has been used from Roman times to the Second World War as an observation post. In addition to the remains of the building, the crowded summit now has an informative viewpoint indicator.

Samlesbury Hall, Samlesbury: The first Samlesbury Hall was destroyed in a raid by Robert the Bruce but was rebuilt in 1325. Over the years it has been a school, pub and factory, and when it was about to be demolished it was saved by the Samlesbury Hall Trust, which has run the building since 1925. It is now used as a visitor attraction.

Forestry debris, Longridge Fell

The Vale of Chipping, Parlick and Fair Snape Fell, Longridge Fell: Longridge is apparently the most southerly fell in the country and there are no prizes for guessing what it looks like from afar. Don't be put off by the extensive plantations on the southern slopes for it is still a fascinating place, and the views are among the best in the county, looking across the verdant Vale of Chipping towards the Bowland Fells.

Vibrant bilberry and the Forest of Bowland, Longridge Fell

Preston to the sea

Wet sand, Big sky, Lytham

The Ribble Way, Tun Brook Wood: Together with Boilton and Red Scar Wood, Tun Brook forms one of the largest areas of semi-natural ancient woodland in Lancashire and is a designated SSSI. The woodland is managed by the Wildlife Trust of Lancashire, Manchester and North Merseyside, who are also developing the gravel pits at Brockholes into an extensive nature reserve and visitor centre.

*Boardwalk, Boilton
Wood*

Rush hour on the M6, Preston: Well, technically it's not quite rush hour as the traffic is moving! Opened in 1958, this section of the M6 - known then as the Preston by-pass – was the first motorway in the country.

Tom Finney, Deepdale: Deepdale, home of Preston North End FC, is the oldest football ground in England and also home to the National Football Museum. Tom Finney spent his entire career at Preston and is regarded as one of the greats of the game.

Harris Museum, Preston: Preston has numerous fine architectural features but without doubt the finest is the Harris Museum. (Courtesy of the Harris Museum)

Receding tide, Mudbanks, Freckleton: The banks of the river at low tide are a muddy quagmire best left to the wading birds.

Riversway Marina, Preston

Riversway Marina, Preston: Preston Docks is the largest single constructed basin in Europe, and traffic through the port reached its peak in the late 1960's. However, within 10 years the business was no longer viable and inevitably it has been redeveloped for residential apartments, offices, shops and pleasure craft.

Brickcroft Nature Reserve, Longton: Three large ponds and woodland now cover the site of the old brickworks in Longton. The long exposure in the dark conditions records some of the atmosphere, but what the camera fails to capture are a dozen long-tailed tits flitting between the trees, a squirrel scurrying from branch to branch, the sound of distant moorhens, and three garrulous jays.

Ribble Way, Longton: The Ribble Way starts at the Dolphin pub, situated at the end of a long dead-end lane near Longton. The path soon takes to the large banks that keep Longton Marsh at bay, before heading towards Preston.

Marsh channel, Longton: The marsh consists of lush pasture and a maze of channels feeding the River Douglas just before it joins the Ribble. A big sky is useful when photographing such a flat landscape.

Passing rain, Longton

Sprouts, Hesketh Bank: The name Hesketh is of Viking origin and has been attributed to meaning either 'landing place' or 'race track' (horse racing having taken place on the sands). Much of the surrounding land has been reclaimed from the estuary and it is now predominantly a market gardening area.

Michaelmas daisies, Marshside

Windmill and lifeboat station, Lytham: It's hard to believe but the windmill was regarded as an industrial eyesore in the 1860s – how times change!

Damp morning, Lytham
jetty, Lytham

Sunset, Lytham Boatyard, Lytham

Twilight tractors, Lytham

Lytham Hall, Lytham: Built in the mid-eighteenth century, this fine Georgian hall was acquired for the town thanks to a huge donation from British Aerospace. Now managed by the Heritage Trust for the North West, it has become an increasing focal point for events.

Dunes, Lytham St. Anne's: The dunes between Lytham and St Anne's are a haven for colourful wildflowers during the summer.

Quiet morning, St Anne's Pier, Lytham St Anne's: A shadow of its former self, St Anne's Pier was shortened following a couple of serious fires in the 1970s and 80s. The soft gentle light summed up this quiet, upmarket seaside town – no over the top drama wanted here.

INDEX

Page numbers refer to captions to the illustrations

PHOTOGRAPHY NOTES

The majority of the photographs were taken on a Mamiya 7II rangefinder camera using either a 65mm or 43mm wide-angle lens. It is a relatively compact and light medium format camera that is suited to landscape work. Several images were taken on an Ebony RSW45, an 'old-fashioned' large format camera that takes 5in x 4in sheet film, using either a Nikon 90mm or 135mm lens. All film stock was Fuji Velvia 50 (old and new). I still use film because I still get excited about being able to hold a transparency that came to life when the shutter was opened – it is a tangible connection to the moment that I was trying to capture and has a magical beauty all of its own. Having said that, a few images were taken on a Nikon D200 DSLR, when the circumstances necessitated.

Other equipment used includes a Manfrotto 055MF3 tripod, with a 410 geared head, and a set of Lee filters. Graduated neutral density filters are absolutely essential when shooting on film as they enable both the sky and land to be correctly exposed – the majority of photographs in the book have utilised an ND grad. All equipment was carried in a LowePro Phototrekker backpack.

If you have any questions about the book please do not hesitate to contact me through my website – www.andylatham.co.uk

In a desire to put something back into the land, ten per cent of the royalties that I receive for sales of the book will be donated equally between the Wildlife Trust for Lancashire and The Yorkshire Dales Millennium Trust for the work they carry out in the Ribble valley. For further information on their work please visit their websites:

www.lancswt.org.uk

www.ydmt.org

ACKNOWLEDGMENTS

In no particular order – Bill and Margaret Brunt for the loan of their caravan; Richard Whitehouse at Lytham Hall and Heritage Trust for the North West for permission to photograph Lytham Hall and Sawley Abbey; The Harris Museum; Whalley Abbey; Tony Baker at the RSPB; the walking guidebooks to the Ribble of Paul Hannon, Dennis and Jan Kelsall and Jack Keighley; Ordnance Survey Explorer maps; my editor Roly Smith for his advice and guidance; the Outdoor Writers' and Photographers' Guild; Peak Imaging; Paul Roper at Johnsons Photopia; and finally to Michelle for all her support. Thank you.